Girl Again

A transformational journey

Christine Madline Ellsworth

Potter's Wheel Publishing House
Minneapolis

Girl Again by Christine Madline Ellsworth

Published by POTTER'S WHEEL PUBLISHING HOUSE
MINNEAPOLIS
MN 55378

www.POTTERSWHEELPUBLISHING.com

© 2020 Christine Madline Ellsworth

All rights reserved. No part of this publication may be reproduced, stored in a retrieval system, or transmitted, in any form or in any means – by electronic, mechanical, photocopying, recording or otherwise – without prior written permission, except as permitted by U.S. copyright law.

"Out of Line" first appeared in The Talking Stick, Volume 22 2013 (Christine Madeline Holm)
"Rembrandt's Light" first appeared in Red Weather, Issue 36, 2017
"Kitchen Table" first appeared in The Talking Stick, Volume 29, 2020

For permissions contact:
info@POTTERSWHEELPUBLISHING.com
Cover by Maduranga Nuwan

ISBN: 978-1-950399-07-9
ISBN: ISBN: 978-1-950399-08-6 (Ebook)
LCCN: 2021932320

To my children, Justin and Alisa;
you two are the loves of my life.

The first poem I wrote, at 17,
was about you--before I even knew you.

Introduction

The large majority of the poems in this book have been with me for decades; I wrote them and rewrote them and edited them again and again until they became new poems with their own identity apart from the original.

Some are brand new and fresh...but they all fit together in a life lived in a woman's body at the turn of the century. Some women may see themselves as "small goddesses" of the sandbox; others may recognize themselves as walking up that endless staircase in the chase for better software.

And if you're lucky enough to have reached your sixth decade---well, I say, welcome. We have earned this place, we women; we have earned the magic we possess allowing us to keep finding the path rising up under our feet.

Contents

Introduction v
Out of Line 1
Black Day 2
First Love 3
A Yi 4
The Geometry of Mystery 9
Ursa Major 11
Half Mile Prayer 13
Embouchure 14
Misnomers 15
Rembrandt's Light 16
From a Defeated Position 19
Reference: Shakespeare's Sonnet #17 20
Précis 21
The Casual Violinist 24
Girl 26
The Power of Invisibility 27
In Favor of Fire 33
Field Work 35
Fossil 36
The Birds of Hong Kong 38
Porch Light 39
Altrui 40
Madeline 41
Wild Peonies 43

Kitchen Table 44
The Rise and Fall of Estrogen 46
Victoria Heals Herself 48
Transplated 49
The Finer Things in Life 50
From 58
Acknowledgement 59

Out of Line

Printed words are bound to lie
Flat, deadtrapped in dry ink on arid paper plains.
They heap up in lines, cracked, rigidblack,
Deserts to confound the furrower's blade and seed
So meaning blows off the top like dust, chaff, lies.

As when I was a willful child to be scolded, I am out of line.
Let me sing inkless and clear on a high blue sky,
Until the words fall, unbinding themselves
As the lines winnow down, free,
Reverting to simple fluid sound.

Black Day

Started out as laundry day.
We had been playing Mother, May I?
in the kitchen on the checkerboard floor
until it started quaking under the spinning Speed Queen
And her sudden shriek, above me, shook the air

Her face soon a mess of mascara and smeared lipstick,
She prayed Hail Mary's in front of the black-and-white portable
that later grayly murmured "Oswald," who, my mother cried,
was *pink*.

The white dryer remained silent, cold, unmoved.

As the World Turned that day in November 1963,
We couldn't watch the soaps.
We didn't dry the clothes.

She wouldn't let me color.
She said it was a black day.

First Love

I had a habit (they called it bad behavior)
then of waking up early and going outside
Sometimes naked (no one knew how or why,
least of all me).
They often found me that way in the sandbox
Making little silica worlds with my own hands,
Eyes down, intent, humming softly:
Small goddess at sunrise.

Or else all the way down by the garage
Where the old, iron swing set stood like a giant saw horse.
I couldn't get on it without stronger, older arms.
But still, I'd push the wooden seats
Seeing the imaginary monster friend,
Blue eyed, smiling back at me.
We laughed.

It was a morning much like that, in my fourth year,
When I looked up, trying to find the hand that
Tickled and shivered the spring leaves on the trees.
I saw for the first time, gazing up—and up
And up 'til I saw you!
I knew I was seeing my first
Love that is with me still, some sixty years gone:
Sky stays with me always.

A Yi

You may not have met him yet, but you know him well:
He's the glassy, storefront motionshape
Occupying the outer third of your out-there, up-here
Range of vision on the new vista of monetized mall mazes.

And you may not see him, even though you, yourself, wear specs
With enough mirror or blue-blocker to know better or
Maybe you just squint deconstructively
And shade your peripheral vision with a salute to tinted power windows,
But A Yi never doubts that, one day, you'll plug into
His higher power with all the omniscience of
Fiber optics and 5G ultrawide with enough gigs to download the Louvre, if you like.
New droids, domains, 3D printers—all for under a thou.

The movies used to call him Hal,
But you know his real name—it's in all the apps, sites and games you buy,
Sprung from the same marketing principles
As whoever dreamed up Uneeda Biscuit.
He's the algorithmic demiurge spawned of the generation
Who played with those primary-colored plastic boxes
Containing bells to ring, knobs to pull, dials to finger, and mirrors to ogle, those
Primitive matrices of one and naught and naught and one.

But you're both grownup now, and you've paid your Gate-money and
So you (and he [even though he's way ahead of you])
consume—assured of the sought-after insight, via
The tantalum/microchip/biogenic/hypertextually.RAMmed Tower of babble that you log onto each morning upon awakening:

A Yi.

There, you sip the heady wine John Galt transposed
From the simple rusted water of Ayn Rand's Iron Age.
There, you skim a complication of encryptions reduced to a sketch of words
Neuroning around ideas trussed so light and framed so cold
They fit on the point
Of a pin.

Fast.
Shiny.
Mercuric.
Mysterious.
Expensive.
Dense indexed.
Blockchained.

You're likely not aware
You've been conditioned to want it.
But you've been empowered to want it.

You attempt to approach it now that you're fully updated to specs
And functioning optimally but he's moved, again

~motionshape~

Again you need the newest version to gain visual access,
a process that repeats itself on your mobius-stripped strings
Upon streamed cloud computations, on its way to the bank.

Multiple chat bots, malware detections and
Ransomed hacks hence, you find yourself
On the escalator attempting to gain footing in the glass-ceilinged,
Escherized software store.
You smile into the arms-length camera.
Again. Hit Send. Hit Like. Hit Angry. Hit Care. Hit Sad.

So now, you have such power that to hit in the virtual realm
Has enough power to kill young girls if they're brown or black;
To decimate Ecuadorians seeking asylum,
To imagine you have enough power to fuck Mother Nature.

But if you're lucky
(or female; if you remember the old witches and prophets)
You can, with a single, metaphysical thought

—crash

                    through—

Catching on elemental fire upon reentry into the atmosphere.

Be forewarned: Your glasses will striate and singe.
Your contacts will shrink and harden.
Your mirrors will craze and crack.
Your nose and your ears and hands will bleed
And you'll drop like stock at its *pasticcio* feet.

You may find yourself feeling amazed:
It looks real, if scripted: The sky has regressed to the historic
First Mac background gray
—or is it steeled for snow?
Is the atmosphere choking in ashes of redwoods?

Listen: A Yi's humming to itself.
Hear the little bubbles of notes
Wobble up as if from an old man's loose-fleshed throat.
His eyes are blue under an age-film of blear yellow.

Surprised, you discern the man it was:
Suppress the urge to smirk at those wiry eyebrows
Sticking out in Einstein equations,
And the silvery, Tesla tufts radiating from such trumpian ears while
That bezos nose appears to be running.

Then as you gingerly push yourself up
From the soggy turf with your shard-shredded hands,
Shivering, you remember a myriad color of clouds
leaves of grass in a welter

Abaty Tyndyrn
The Luddite rebellion of 1811 because,
Remember, User,
You were lucky.

With this realization,
you see the sky has grown portentously darker:
Overhead one flap then two fold brownly down.

Leap, now, in one brilliant, motionshaped thought of

~out~!

See, now, its shrunken frame still stirring
The puddle of pixilated water with the staff-like stick
Until it hydrologically whorls and twists the screensaver landscape like a sodden rag

First sucking out water, next grass and whole trees,
Adumbral roots, then mud and a haul of rocks and sludge.

The tenebrific flap folds,
And just before you tuck the fourth under a corner of the first
And blot the box with the sales receipt for its return,

A Yi looks up to say:

"Once, there were enough stars to see the lamplighter's breath on a cold, clear night;
A time dim enough to glimpse paradise.
Don't forget to turn the lights off before you leave."

The Geometry of Mystery
(For Darla)

She was out
Seventeen
on a run early morning
Spring day
Dirt road

He was out
Checking soil
Old farmer
Spring day
Tilling fields

Comes upon
a mystery:
Pond draining fast
Fish leaping
Fish drowning
In air

He runs home
Grabs buckets
Runs back
To the disappearing
Pond
Grabs fish

Fills bucket
After bucket
Runs over the hill
Dumps them
Into the deep lake
Alive

She rounds the curve
Sees the old farmer
The buckets
The mystery
In front of her

Enters the pond
Grabs a bucket
Plucks up fishes
Totes uphill
Dumps them
Into the deep lake
Alive

After an hour
It is done
The fish and the water
Are gone
And we none of us
Know where our blessings
Come from

Ursa Major

No fluid;
All is ice at forty below.
It's said such cold
Can freeze lungs midsentence.
Outside, the lake heaves---
The long-cemented reverberations
Of the tons of ice ramming against a hidden shoreline---
A bear's growl, an echoed shard in the otherwise
Frigid, crystalline void.
Here, there is no heat, no blood, no life.
Only the midwinter's blank arc, the sapless snap of pine,
A sighing, forgetful healing of mercury,
A ptarmigan's white-winged sleep.

Stung awake, I go out into that black abyss---
Swathed and swaddled in fabrics design to trap heated molecules close---
Down a bladed, half-mile lane then east,
Up a wide hill of deer-stripped stalks.
Already my toes are harder, heavier, the blood forced inward.
If I was in love, the moment would be enough to keep me alive,
Like the doe lodged down in the marsh, curled around next spring's fawns—

But his cold trail, left green months and soft rains earlier
Feeds a fire so far afield the pain cracks worse than deepest winter
And leads me out to cool, and hunt the savage answer.
There, the constellations wheel silently, turning on some splintered axis
More ancient than our bones or blood.
I scan the seven shiny mirrors and mark the bear's high silence.
Yet my breath is,
Rises.

Half Mile Prayer

The waters rise
and the snows recede that you may stir
soon after an occlusion of ice but prepare:
A half mile before the break
hear the tumble
Of white noise
Teased, frothed foam
Flailing and hurling
Over the sleek, ancient boulders.
Thunder obliterates thought
The closer you come
Drenching and pummeling
The prayer from your soul
Until you stand in the spray
Wet with rebirth

Embouchure

Clear water breath
Sings water like sugar
Hived sugars swarm
Flows water clear

Swallow,
Breathe.

White fire sweats
Mineral black salt deep
Twice twist impressed
Sweats white fire

Sweat salt breath
Embrace spiced taste
Burnt sugar split
Twain clear waters

Breathe,
Swallow.

Water stars flow
Shine twist sugar
Stars shine sing water
He sings chords in my throat.

Misnomers

Falcon-gentle
Hunts, poor sport
Photographic crop
On her prey aloft
Glides noiseless
Cockatrice eyes
Brilliant and merciless
Wings rigged like a net
Poised for the clenched spoils
Her disembowelled
Vermillioned trophies
Savaged midair
Break-neck
Who, but humankind, named her so?

Rembrandt's Light

A #4 pencil
Drew his dark things:
Hand-rubbed shadows in the hollow parts of breastbone, lip, and temple;
Blackened blurry questions marks that pocked the bedroom walls, and
Rows of daggery dots sketched hastily across inverted exclamation points
So heavily graphited that they dully pewterize.

It was a fine tool for slashing, too:
Serrated the rumpled black-eyed page
—my jagged rip, tear and shred—
Distorted axis lines detailed a cross-hatched hard edge,
Punctured and drained the living tint of human skin.

But it was, finally, snapped into
The back of an institutionally pink room,
Where he took drawing lessons in a thin gown;
Was the used-up eraser and splintered piece
With the counter-sunk to bare-wood molar marks that he put there, himself.
They calmly presented clean rag stock and a sharpened #2;
Expected illuminations—promised me pastels.

Came years, then, of the slow divergence from that old master:
Some time hiding in hotels and in lights-out rental cars on backstreets,
Disappearing in broad daylight in between the stark lines of realism.
Later came the court rooms lined with young lawyers
Brandishing their letters of metallic legalese in the days of carbon-copied records,
That slurry of pigments winding through offices in an Escherized procession---
One hand shaking another yet attached at a common source:
There was no true perspective in those pen-and-ink times.

Later still, I took up with the postmodernity of green polymers and wet acrylics,
Impressionistic streaks of cerise, some inspirations of celadon,
And, ever bolder-hued, advanced into blocks of Mondrian order,
Despite more pencils, pens, and brushes with abstraction.

When Rembrandt's light dawned plain and simple in my fifty-seventh year—
Like a shade lifted from the window of my dim study—
This muddy, sensuous slip of earth finally settled in a true proportion
As under the steady, hot heat of a wood-fired kiln.
I came to know this new element slowly, quietly and greenly,
Like a tree budding in the earth on a hard spring,
Through a season of soft, holy rains and waving grasses,

Through a shimmer of autumn leaves aloft on its illuminating radiance,

Then—these many years later—it transformed those shadows, silhouettes, and surfaces

Into this clear-eyed movement of easy coursing blood and balanced feet,

Wholly free form, shine-faced: A girl, again, with a broom.

From a Defeated Position

She is crouched
She is a violated fold of legs and arms
She is downed

She is numb
She is collapsed
She is breathless but takes in

An upwelled breath
She blinks
She unlocks a fist

She rolls her weight back upon her heels
Braces one thigh muscle then the other
And hauls the whole of herself up onto her feet

And so stands.
She slowly unlocks the other fist
And brings both palms together

Then flings wrists wide
And opening her mouth
Sings a victory of soft stars into the night sky

Reference: Shakespeare's Sonnet #17

You are mistaken, Dr. Hudson—
Words be the ancient, gummy glue
Holding worlds, like hands, together—
Syllabic planets "Me" and "You."
You are mistaken, Dr. Hudson,
If you think this is not true:
Your linguiscience solipsizes
Yourself, not II or 2 or *deux*.
Your are mistaken, Dr. Hudson
If you propound such likes.
Strabisimus makes truthes unclear
And wipes word-wiseness from your eyes:
Our language—writ or spake—it ties
One mind unto another; the proof? Begat, you read these lines.

Précis

No, it's best you don't.
Because if you did,
I would waste your time asking you
To hum the twelve songs you sing,
Trying to touch a place on your throat where
I could snatch your voice in my bare hand
To hide in my imaginative verses.
I would ask you way too many questions
Like, Do you like Boccherini?
Have you ever fingerpainted on windowpanes
Or would you like to? And, What, then,
is best?
Such nonsense as this would only distract you.

I'd probably get much too personal
If you did,
Reading your thoughts over your shoulder
Just when you'd rather read them to an audience.
I might make you madder than hell
If I attacked your precious Pound (but only
To feel your heavy pencil strokes
On my paper) and since
You've been to Ireland and Mexico and Greece
Where you drank
Lethean Elsewhere
Until you were stumbling down drunk

And I've only been to Fargo
My Frostian notions would cool that liquid high
Like *The Emperor Of Ice Cream* doled out in snow shovels.
You'd be exasperated, insulted, perhaps pissed
But tension would be real.

And you would say a great many things
I wouldn't understand, being untaught;
Although if they were about modern art
I wouldn't listen anyway—
I'd think, instead, about those faces
You probably make in the mirror in the morning
When you shave—
You'd be talking Monet
While I'd picture me gently wiping soap
From your soft upper lip, and putting my cheek then,
To yours:
White towel, pink light, mist glass
Blurred a bit leafy from summer outside.
You'd be so distracted you'd stop
Trying to find the lines where I hid your voice.

But if you did,
The biggest surprise, of course,
Would be discovering we once both weeded tomato patches
and like the sweaty work and the green vine tang
on our fingers, and the red squishy flavor of them warm from the sun.
We'd probably get hungry, remembering this,
And would want to go somewhere to eat.

Right away.
Then, you'd like me too much and too easily
With my white slip flowering from under my skirt—
And especially if we sang three or four flutes of Dom
You might find yourself saying
That I was
—o, yes—
developing
poetically.

I might even convince you to go driving
Out in the country with me, after all,
out to the highest point in Blue Earth county
Where I'd show you a chain of seven lakes
Laying wide and quiet under starlight
Like sheets of cracked glass smashed in a midnight fire:
My Elsewhere.
You'd be moved by the sight and silence up there,
And you might even kiss me
(to thank me)
But you,
—being married—
Would have to go.
Probably suddenly.

No, no, no; not to her, I mean:
But to the place where we put our glasses back on
And count out syllables
For a living.

The Casual Violinist

Too much job, too much commuting, too much calendar
Begets the silence of bow, the stillness of strings.
The casual violinist often feels too much life
As a log jam of notation
Backing up to her forearms.
Withheld expression through string or key
Brings on the long-term blockage resulting in
Songs pushing up into her biceps
Scaling shoulders and neck –
Within weeks
Musculature, tabulature, and instrument
have all gone to sleep.

The violin is brought to a beautiful, renowned Saint Paul luthier,
Possessing patience and expense, sonatas and fugues in his hands
Who will replace pegs and tail piece, pull the soundpost
Lift the top and clean the insides, scrape old glue,
Caliper ebony nuts, flatten patches and cleats
Graphite certain slots, fit a new Aubert bridge.
Until it has been cleaned and wiped and oiled and loved and refitted
Into a new song called Hold.

The casual violinist can be found a few blocks away
In the chain music store eyeing the Harps,
And the men with long hair
Tapping her feet; well--
Shoulda known better with a girl like you.

Girl

They said you are a girl.
You can't do what we do.
You don't think like we do.
You aren't strong.
You can't go there.
You can't come in here.

They said how did you do that?
Who said you could?
How did you figure it out?
How did you fix that engine, that leak, that fire, that theorem, that prayer?
How did you move that range, that plastic, that stock, that church?

I am a girl.
We all begin phenotypically female.
We are you.
You are us.

The Power of Invisibility

I was on my hands and knees,
crawling over terrain that had been ravaged.
It was clear water had leveled the earth:
there were no trees, no roads, no houses—only a defiled substance over which I moved.
Looking down at it, I could discern bits of tree bark, seeds, shreds of cloth and curls of metal, and small chunks of asphalt blended unharmoniously into a crusty layer baked by long days of sun.
After the flood.

I knew where I was, though.
I was making my way up a hill,
up to the family farm that my father had bought forty years ago.
The farm, dotted with red apple and plum trees,
rimmed Sand Lake, and sat atop one of the highest points in the county.
It was a small island now—Sand Lake was gone—and the house, the barn,
the ancient oak tree in the front yard were all that was left.
Along with me.

Reaching the top of the hill where the flood scum gave way,
I was able to stand on shaky legs.
I turned around to face what was once rolling hills of corn

and wheat and fenced fields filled with cows bounded by gravel roads.
Now, I saw only the baked muddy remnant of the flood waters and the formlessness
of what could no longer be called a landscape.
Violent storms, capable of such devastation, I thought, must have raged for some time.
The flood waters may have swirled in the area—
host long ago to the ancient Lake Agassiz, that remnant of the melting glaciers of the Ice Age—
for years before receding, leaving this sediment to bake
in seasons of sun so long, it was like the Earth had turned inside out or upside down.

I'd heard of that; science posited the magnetic poles of the Earth
shifted once every millennia or so. Is this what had happened?
The air brought no pleasant scent.
Not a blade of grass, not a road, not a lake, not another house or barn or car or cow anywhere.
There was still a horizon, where the land met the sky.
There was still a sun in the sky. There was a bee buzzing somewhere.
(Miracles hide everywhere.)
The farm still stood. And I had survived.
I blinked at the devastation all around me.
I had survived, but I was alone.

And then, of course, a whirlwind plucked me up
out of that netherworld, and I opened my eyes. It had been a dream,
and there was the flood of relief at finding myself in a warm,
soft bed in a house I owned in a county poised
on the edge of the April planting season.
The faint light of early dawn peeked shyly into my bedroom windows,
and I could hear the birds singing in the neighborhood treetops.
Slowly, I smiled. Thank you, I thought. Thank you.
You know the feeling:
You have an awful dream, and it feels so real, you are living it.
Joy is so heightened the angels come swiftly. The anger so vehement it bleeds from your pores and you say a hex of horrid corrosions to unsuspecting people in that altered reality.
And the fear—the fear so pervasive and acute you are unable to scream through a wide-open mouth or move on legs that have turned to trees rooted down to deep lithosphere.
So that when you wake up, you are filled with joy all over again at being here, in your imperfect world.
Even if it is this world of impending environmental doom, cataclysmic contagion with its devastation of truth, which can make dreams seem preferential.

In that other world,
Many dreams, we're told, are fear-based and, true enough,
they seem to have been since I was small.
Did you ever dream of giants?
How about scary giants lurking in the dark depths of your closet?

I remember being about five when I had that dream.
Now that I think about it, it probably signifies how scary the adults (giants)
can be and puzzling (in the dark)
and also sort of secretive (closet).
Sure, this is the adult me interpreting a child's dream.
But I'd say that by the time we are five, we have already internalized
some fairly sophisticated stuff, like being puzzled by someone's behavior.
And being secretive may come naturally to us as a species.

I recall stuffing handfuls of my dinner I couldn't eat but was expected to (at three)
into the pockets of my robe. I do not know where I got this brilliant idea.
I thought it was brilliant then, and I do today, too. Never got caught.
When I shared this childhood story with a hairy coworker in Milwaukee,
He nodded.
He said he used to sneak bits of his dinner into the curly depths of his hair.
His parents never discovered it, although he may have left a trail
His pet poodle enjoyed.
Often when you're small,
You're used to being below the line of sight in the adult world of giants.
(As are many pets.)

It's good training. Later, when you live in a city, you're often used to being mostly invisible
in the giant world of buildings.
Being mostly invisible is a fabulous power we use as humans.
It helps when you're out among people:
You move along, undetected, in a crowd.
You pay attention to the rules—stay in the proper walking lanes,
don't make eye contact,
don't draw attention to yourself—
and you'll pass like a droplet of clear water flowing downstream.

So you slip into a store, buy a red dress, leave the store with a bag
and get on the bus or train and exit at your stop.
You walk up the stairs to your apartment.
And it all happened without anyone saying anything to you
except the thanks you were given at the register,
for which you are grateful; look how quickly you got the shopping done!

It isn't good to be too invisible for too long, though.
Take this year.
A year of impending environmental doom, cataclysmic contagion, with its devastation of truth, which can make dreams seem preferential.
If you string too many days together without contact or resistance in the flow or even just locking eyes with another human being, you start wondering if you're real.

If no one can see you, you may not be, comes the sad and scary thought.

So when I fell in love with that man, it was because he saw me this morning,

Standing in my red dress at the bus stop under an umbrella in the rain,

even while wearing a mask.

In Favor of Fire

No swinger of birches, here
in this boneyard of jagged boughs broken trunks
and the fibulas long askew
or those bandaged by pale, powdery lichen.

No, these relics from a more oxygenated day now
Defy view, deter rambles, stop seedlings.

In the Boreal they wait, breathless and bated,
For a catalyst of air or the mean strike of Thor,
Their latent arms an enthalpy of lignin and cobwebs--
Silent matters in stilled, blighted leaves—
blackened skeletons of canker and scales
Overripe for the random kiss of combustion.

Our beloved white paper birch, too long aground undisturbed but revered,
Naturally sicken and die, bowing like tired, overburdened old men;
Tumble earthward, their exposed root balls astonish as the toes would of wraiths
Whose gnarled limbs ache and shrivel, succumbing to bearded mosses
And break, conquered quietly in a heartless labyrinth of protected decay.

While Superior lakeshore memories, matchless, turn sullen,
The boys of the '50s, looking up at their grandfathers, those Boundary Waters men
With their high-held wood paddles weeping soft drops like a lash to the eye,
Will no longer cast dreams aloft
on blue skies made bluer by the storied, white treetop.

No swinger of birches.
No heavenly climb.
The trees can bear no more.

Field Work

Years ago, I'd shrug on his Realtree snow-camouflage jacket
Wearing nothing else under but a trace of bare limbs, a quiver of flesh.
Then, he hunted me savagely, soft-mouthed on hot wetlands wild beyond ken.

In time, came a winter of deep snows and dishonor too heavy for shrugging or shrift,
And he—befouled and untethered, too late for amends—came loping along
On the trail of my prints, swollen by hours, nose down on a dimming of bright turning brown.

That jacket, I imagine, still hangs on the hook where I left it, unwashed and yellowing slowly.
His prescriptions no longer give rise to those memories, or for his failing memories of her.
He drifts naked and hollow—full body decoy—afraid of flushing our lingering scent.

Fossil

Hard-hearted sludge and thick grit do not long reside motionless
Or alone but silt slowly together in slurries of ache and
Aggregate, whip upwind the chinook in a knurl of waves,
Skiff swiftly back down under cold-knuckled riverbeds
to submerge in a ghost of untrue turbidity.

Such vexed, dirty sediment, subsumed under sunlight,
Impresses, like unvoiced grievances, deep down
Into weighty, miles-wide geographical faults
And takes shape—out among the temblor—
Involute, spiraling, undammed anger solidifies. Hardens.
Ceases.

Now, no summons or chant can abridge or relay
Our echoing interstices among drained estuaries—
Those sinkholes of prayer falling straight down to clay.
Our words evaporate, hard as runes amid fanned dorsal fins
Implied upon ancient plains rising volcanic,
To compound in new abstracts of question, conjecture
—was it true? Did we warriors once hold hands in the garden?

Many dawns from that day in the courtroom
A fresh-faced child spies the blood-colored stone, plucks it up
from the shore;
Squints at our curious incisions and scrolls, rolls his thumbs
over a tangle of fissures

That utter mere whispers of a past–ours–he can't fathom. A mystery!
And so with a sudden snap of joy, he flings the stone far out
Over a calm, clean lake where it skips happily, sinks freely and
Rocks slowly down—safe lullaby—into the forgiving arms of the Earth.

The Birds of Hong Kong

There, on my Zoom screen, is a poet in China.
She introduces herself by her two names:
The English is sweetly sibilant but
the Cantonese sounds sweeter,
More musical, Ēndiǎn.
And, when she shares it in writing,
It's beautiful, strong, balanced as she: 恩典 Grace

Behind her, a bay.
The sky is clear, is blue.
It is fresh. Not as I'd been trained to see it at all—
Black and white on the pages of a sad, flat school book.

She reads a poem in front of an open window
Twenty stories up.
The birds in Hong Kong join with her voice,
Become one in a hanzi of
Logogramic sound:
Chànggē 唱歌 singing
Niǎolèi 鳥類 birds
Hé 和 and
Shīgē 和 poetry

Porch Light

Airborne at night over northernmost continents,
See the far ranging starlight ignite shifting clouds
And emanate outward, Magellan-like, massive,

Effloresce, spraying drops of spilled mirror
That cluster and collide, falling soundless
Into the immeasurably distant, dark arms of space.

Later, after landing, when the garage door closes
And the porch light flips quietly on the pre-dawn dew,
See the soft, luminous flux spread a single foot candle in our still yard.

And your smile, behind the opening door, is a galaxy, too.

Altrui

If your strength is in your legs,
First walk behind then beside
Soon perhaps, ahead
Until you outdistance yourself and unhinder us

If your strength is in your money
Give it away. What energy is in paper?
Paper burns fast so wick.
Put your power in its source: the tree

If your strength is in your vision
Read by candlelight then
Cleans lens sclera and see in direct
Starlight the earth's day and your own conjunctiva

If your strength is in your voice
Call it up breath in song
Strum sugar salt acid
Enough to fill the belly our lungs

Madeline

I was in a little wooden boat with a friend
On Pearl Lake in northern Minnesota.
It was Mother's Day—or Memorial Day—I can't remember.

We fished lazily, for Northern, snagging a string
Of juveniles that afternoon, releasing them back over the side.
Taking a breather, I cast a hand in the water, looking up to stare down the sky.

Soon the sky started talking, widening into words,
speaking the name "Madeline." The name of the grandmother on my mother's side, the French one, is what the sky said.

It said this by billowing up huge, scallopy clouds
Tossing them onto the barest of bluenesses,
And whistling them all in a brisk, northerly wave. The boat rocked.

"Madeline died when I was only six," I said to my fisherfriend, as if translating, "so I don't remember much about her.
At my age, I looked up to her. She was rounded, soft, white-haired.

"The day she died, I didn't understand death
As I do now but, being told that I would never see her again,
I understood she had become invisible (a superpower), though

Never to share fresh cookies with us from the old orange
Coffee can, or offer sun-ripened tomatoes plucked new
From the vine, still warm in the deep well of her clean, white apron

Or to sit on the sagging planks, porchgazing at sunset
With her watery, french-blue eyes, shelling green peas. I know nothing else of her
Except what my mother said once, years later:

"'She weeded the garden the day she died. She had 11 children.
Two died of diphtheria. She whistled comforting airs at times when
Most wives would break down.' This is all of remember of her."

My fisherfriend nods, wisely quiet. He sees the same lake and sky,
But doesn't hear the same woman as I do; of course not—for I
Myself, only hear her on days when the mirror is round with white clouds

Just as it was the day she died. I remember my grandmother,
Not in the small things a child knew of her, but in the big lensing
Of shine she has become, above and below, between lake and sky.

We drifted on Pearl Lake, listening.

Wild Peonies

Too much love ungiven greens ardent
In the sugar-veins of new leaves
Flinging raised palms in prayer to shuttered skies
While the secret-packed, ant-dense, pink-streaked buds clamp
Fist-tight to arm-wrestle and toss through a cold, dim June

Burst July eighth, hang heavy and heat-ripe for the shears and vase
A magnificence of fragrant clouds, soft as earthbound angels
Sweeping pale pearly ears against the dew for the turn of any footfall,
Fall limply in the breeze sowing petals and pollen in neighboring acres

To sunspot and wrinkle, colorless as an old woman's fingertips
Where they beckon from the black, newly bladed earth
Like a spray of far stars in the scrim of a distant galaxy
Laced bare in a texture of thinned skin and bruised veins

Blown further and further afield each passing summer,
Seeded and varied in pastures more than a mile away,
Gone leggy and spindled amid tall, waving grasses:
Those pink, tended petals resurrect in raw minerals
To become brimful teacups of defiant, wild red.

Kitchen Table

Close cousins drag the family farm table and two chairs
From the perspiring inside out onto the soft July lawn
Nearing moonrise, for a post-picnic talk under the stars
Near a lake in Becker County, Minnesota.
One hand-carved oak leg of the table sinks under an elbow
Pops up with the weight of the other's and
Their spilled chardonnay makes of laughter a leavening.

Within moments the glass pitcher, topped with their icy wine,
Sweats a faint water sheen and sets new dark circles, hastily hand-sopped
but soon enough set in the soft old wood already scarred
with Uncle Sigge's initials the night his sister Linnea arrived in '22,
the soft depression where the weekly bread was kneaded for decades,
and the corduroyed gouges set by the Allis Chalmers Model B engine
Grandpa Josef rebuilt during the harrowing winter of 1947.

This evening, their soft, reverent voices recount the familiar old stories
of beloved godmother Astrid or the stern, hired-hand Pal or
The babies that died of diphtheria and the still that brewed hooch in the '30s
When no grain would grow.

Now, the years' news—the mass shootings, hurricanes, starving Polar bears—

Scares them equally and with their heads close in the dark, the two talk over

The faint, ghostly rings and unclaimed tattoos on the ancient table while overhead,

acorns dance on the Northern Red oaks growing slowly toward the farmhouse rooftop.

The Rise and Fall of Estrogen

Thirteen:
Held thrall
Dirty
Outside reason

Held thrall
Shave legs
Outside reason
Wash blood

Shave legs
Skinned knees
Wash blood
Climb trees

Skinned knees
Invert reason
Climb trees
Fall

Invert reason
Lipstick
Fall
Wash blood

Lipstick
Marry
Wash blood
Bear child

Married
Lose reason
Bear child
Blue heart

Lose reason
Offer mind
Blue heart
Black eye

Offer mind
Wash blood
Black eye
Close knees

Wash blood
Walk legs
Close knees
Sing reason

Walk legs
Unbound
Sing reason
Returned reason

Unbound
Cleanliness
Returned reason
Sixty.

Victoria Heals Herself

Her wide white hips, so remarkable,
Made black men in the streets of Chicago
Turn and stare, take note in hushed ohs
And raised eyebrows when she passed.
She knew they did.
She always said, with that dazzling smile:
Certain men love big hips.

And it does take a discerning gent to
See the strength in her swagger, to see how those hips
Have carried her home, day after day, for more
Than 60 years. Through her childhood in Milwaukee.
Through a marriage (he came out gay). Through
grad school in Indiana, to Norway and back. To
The ritzier suburbs of Chicago.

She be strong.

So when the cancer showed up a second time
The surgeons harvested some subcutaneous treasure
From of those amazing, white hips
And fashioned a new breast for a matching pair.
Victoria healed herself with herself.
Certain men still flirt with their beautiful brown eyes.
She still got her swagger. She still be strong.
She likes to say, with her hands on those wide, white hips:
These babies saved my ass more than once.

Transplanted

I used to be a set of Corelle "Butterfly Gold" plates
Upon which I served red reheated spaghetti
To the delight of my innocent family.
Other times, I was a blue-flowered Delft saucer
Acquired for a buck at a second-hand store to
Contain the day's jewelry or quartz watches.
For one single season, I posed as an inherited
Jean Pouyat hard paste creamer: Limoge.
Was Dainty. Translucent. Expensive. Hand painted.
(But far too easily shattered.)
So most often I was that comfortable, hand-thrown clay mug of hot coffee:
Strong. No sugar, no cream. All business, no play. Jack's indeed a dull boy.

So how is it that now, I've become a broad china tray with two
Smooth, wooden handles, enough room for the plates saucers old mugs and spaghetti
Dollar-store jewelry and watches, the coffee
From fridge-to-bed with no care for the crack of old Wedgewood
Nor the shame of the '70s white bourgeoisie and
Enough spills to keep it regal and real?
Today, yes:
I am all Marilyn
Not the bone porcelain of Spode nor a slim Noritake
But a blond-going-silver, sexy cup C.

The Finer Things in Life

We weren't much alike, my mom and me:
She, Vogue gorgeous;
My looks, she deemed "dramatic."
She, the Homecoming Queen and Valedictorian,
Me, Senior Class President. School newspaper writer.
She, entrepreneurial—developing and managing
Three businesses, one of which is thriving, today.
Me: Itinerant. Vagabond.

I remember telling her when I was 13
I'd live forever.
I meant it. I was serious, sitting there
In the dining room of our Sears catalog
farm home shipped in crates by rail in 1913.
She never broke a smile.
Nodded. Looked me in the eye.
Said: "Okay."

I don't remember her laughing much
(perhaps not inclined with those businesses,
three boys, a vampire daughter,
a husband with PTSD, compliments of Korea).

But--- this one time, coming out of the grocery store---
the cantaloupe bounced up out of the bag
leaping from the cart I was pushing

And rolled down the parking lot, renegade fruit!
We looked at each other. I braced myself:
because usually she'd scowl and say something like,
Chris!
as if I personally created the bumps in the parking lot
just for the mischief of ruining ripe melons.

But this one time, she decided it was funny,
Lifted her head up in a laugh.
I jubilantly fetched it from a pothole and later
we divvied up the slices as dessert, her retelling the story
while we spooned those juicy, orange commas
and slurped, giggling and choking, inhaling the vitamins
contained in her smile.

Me: a Bachelor of Arts, Master of Arts
She: two years at the state university.
Me: still alive, for now. There's a pandemic out there.
She: died in 2004, probably from smoking
Me: I quit. Three years now.

After the funeral, dad gave me a slim packet.
Her stories. What, wait--she was a writer?
"She was proud of you,"
he said, nodding.
"But she was jealous, too.
She wanted to finish college.
She should have finished.
She should have published a book."

Jealous? Mom? Of me?
I scowl.
Now, these many years later,
I page through her stories,
Knowing the we'll never get the time back
To heal, to be closer
The way some mothers and daughters are.
We'd talk about plot, character, tension, resolution;
We'd edit each other, redlining a future.

But, suddenly an idea: *we can* write together; we will.
And so, forthwith: she speaks in *italics*; as such, I do not.

A DEMAND FOR SERIOUS THOUGHT
(title on the cover of a 1940s high school paper)
Art, she posited, *appears to us through medium and elements;*
The medium is evident.
The elements are: line and shape
Value and mass, texture, color, volume, and perspective.
Oil, canvas, fresco, tempera. Iambic, hexameter.
Rhythm, melody, harmony, syncopation.

Hear all these, she says, in the measures of Dvorak, Bach and Brahms.
See them in classics such as "The Birth of Venus", and El Greco's "Resurrection"
(she was schooled by Catholics),
Read them in the verses, prose, and poetry of Milton or Shakespeare.
Music, architecture, painting, literature, we've been taught,
are four of the finer things in life.

But what about the fifth---sculpture?
Employing a writerly trick of transition, she turns to her own mother,
And asks:
Mother, who are some sculptors?
Her answers ensue, each solid line detailing
The everyday architecture of her family life.

Dishwashing to her was a ritual.
Each cup, plate, or dish of pressed green glass, she rinsed individually in steaming hot water.
She would set me on the cabinet beside her
To keep her company.
There I noticed the shelves: Home to the coffee and tea cans,
The red and white salt shakers flanking tins of allspice, cinnamon, nutmeg and cloves
Next the bottles: vanilla, maple, and lemon. Higher up: the aspirin, iodine, nose drops and bandages.
Below, the big bins filled with loose flour and cascading white sugar
Usually so heavy I couldn't open them, myself.

While mother washed dishes she sang songs to me.
Sure, holidays brought the carols. But my favorite was
The Song of Little Joe, whose parents had died:
"No mother to love him/So out in the cold he walked/Poor Little Joe."

Mom, driving to the train station in Deerfield,
In that '65 Galaxy 500, tapping her wedding ring on the steering wheel,

Groovin' on the Monkees' "Last Train To Clarksville."
Soon, there appeared dad, back from the downtown Chicago commute,
Six o'clock analog-sharp with his black briefcase, tan raincoat,
Sliding behind the wheel while she slid over to the passenger side.
I sat, unbelted, in the blue vinyl back seat and watched them kiss
(my head full of Davy Jones).

Mother wasn't sentimental in a sentimental way.
One Sunday after the war had begun and sugar was scarce
She asked me what I'd like to do after church?
Make some fudge! --I selfishly blurted out, quickly embarrassed.
She kissed me just below my widow's peak and said:
"What makes you think you need any more sweetness?"

The snow was raging that day, late December 1970:
Sixty-below-zero morning, a surreal walk
down the half-mile-long driveway to catch the stupid school bus
was the order of my morning. On the radio weather prediction,
Mom had stayed up all night sewing (on a Singer, youbetcha)
A pair of acetate-lined alpaca wool pants--bell-bottoms, no less!
I found them steamed and creased, first thing that dark hour
At the foot of my bed. They were perfect.
They were warm, soft. They were a gift asking
Forgiveness: You must walk this far in the cold,
I am sorry but I know the old truck will not start.

Yeah, I didn't wear them.
At thirteen, everything makes you look fat.
I hang my head to think of this today.
Yet she waved me out the door that morning, just the same, smiling.
And was there in the kitchen with a mug of hot cocoa
when I trudged back up that darkening afternoon.

Mother could sew and knit quite well but found little time
To do these things while all of us children
(my grandma had eleven)
were growing up. Last Christmas,
she knit me a pair of white, woolen stockings.
They were soft and thick with ribbed tops.
Mother said, "I'm afraid I made a few little mistakes.
"We'll have to call them seconds."

She was a rainbow: a stunning chestnut brunette in the 1950s,
Audacious box-red babe in the '60s
and then a natural bleached blond
In Jimmy Carter's 1970s, out in the garden weeding for hours.
By the '90s she was silvery, retired, styled in a professional
Pageboy, once a week and coming off a bit snooty because of it.

If she saw me now, with my side-shaved
boy-cut, fake platinum blond-slash-silver pixie,
she'd probably shake her head even
While privately reassuring herself:
Chris has been married twice

and has two children and three grandchildren.
I know she's not gay but why oh why
Does she want to look like a boy. And what's that
Tattoo on the back of her neck? What a sailor!
And I'd think back at her: Pageboy haircuts were
First worn by pages who were traditionally boys, mom.
Same thing, different century.
It's something certain strong women can pull off.
(The tattoo is a personal connection between me and my son.)

Getting ready for Mass on Sunday morning was always a hub-bub.
She helped everyone find their stockings,
Their second shoe or their prayerbook.
Then she hurriedly combed her long hair
Which was beginning to gray and pulled it to the back
Of her head in a sort of a twist
Fastening it with as many bobby-pins as she had time for
(this, too, the mark of a strong woman).
And after dinner, Mother read the Sunday Funnies to us.
I realize she enjoyed them, herself, because nowadays
She reads one or two out loud even though we all of us
Of course, can read. We always laugh. Thank you, Mother!

The notes in the margins of the teacher who graded mom's paper
Reveal an unimaginative mind: "I don't understand your beginning, your end?
Why quotation marks? What are 'The Finer Things in Life'?
What is the point? Why is paragraph 1 impossible as writing?"

I am surprised, abashed—mom's meaning is quite clear, even brilliant.
No, it wasn't a modern viewpoint.
Back the in '40s, the dust-bowl days were
A part of the poor, farming past we must deny;
Then, the machinations of educational liberalism
had already begun. The daughter of a provincial
Cannot be so bold as to know what she was talking about,
Nor what she was seeing.
Joan concludes:

The five arts, I am told, are:
literature, music, architecture, painting and sculpture.
I've recognized them, I see them everyday in
a story, read aloud
a salt cellar
an imperfect work of white yarn
an old song
a dish of green glass.

Meanwhile, Mother—have we missed
the Finer Things in Life?

From

I come from another place every three or so years
From a father who misread maps
but innocently believed travel begets geography,
and from a mother who wanted to plant

I come from the next town over the next state line
tumbleweed
yet you always find me gathering again
the next round of cardboard boxes
sized somewhere between
the fortified whiskey crates from the local liquor store
and the fruit-stained farmer's market totes
blotted with fresh thumbs of
strawberries like dabs of delight
on a homey plate
of buttered, brown
toast

I come from days that spread out
over everything like direct sunshine sometimes and
others like cold hard Kelvin ice on a cracked windshield
but all of it, up to and including now
this—the real miracle of my life, this--
this path
that keeps on
appearing
under my feet

Acknowledgement

I WISH TO acknowledge the many people who have taught me about the meaning of poetry and what it can do in our lives. Special thanks to:

Geri Chavis, my mentor through the International Federation for Biblio/Poetry Therapy, for being willing to guide me through the process of becoming a Certified Applied Poetry Therapy Facilitator (CAPF), and help me understand the important healing power--and history---of poetry.

Thank you to the entire English department faculty at Minnesota State University Moorhead (several of you actively convinced me to abandon my pre-law major). One even had to give me a failing grade for missing too many evening creative writing classes--as a single mother, I had to work in order to support two young children even though I wanted to write more than anything. It's a fun story and one that makes me smile, even today--because I am still writing. The words will have their way.

www.ingramcontent.com/pod-product-compliance
Lightning Source LLC
Chambersburg PA
CBHW061511040426
42450CB00008B/1564